Thank you!

Thank you so much for purchasing this coloring book!
I hope you absolutely loved it! Be sur to follow
us on Amazon to get updates on new books!

Abella Publishing

Designed by: Abella Publishing

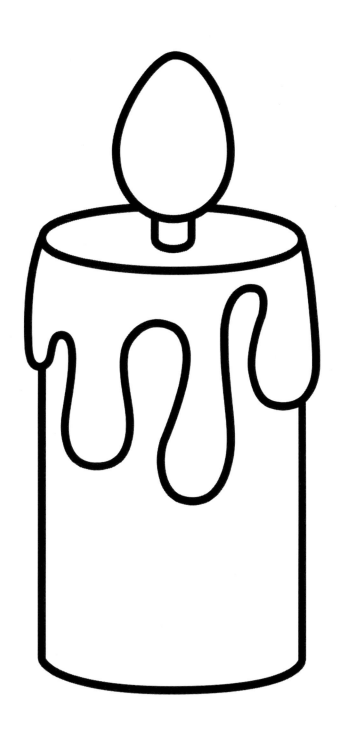

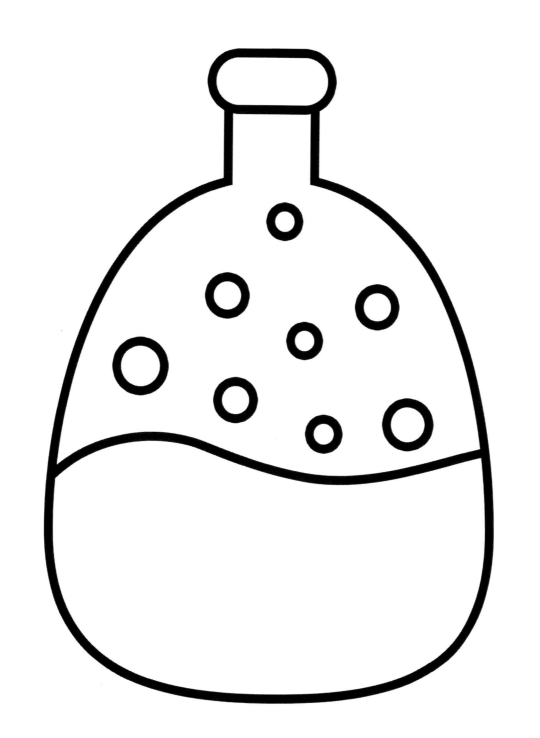

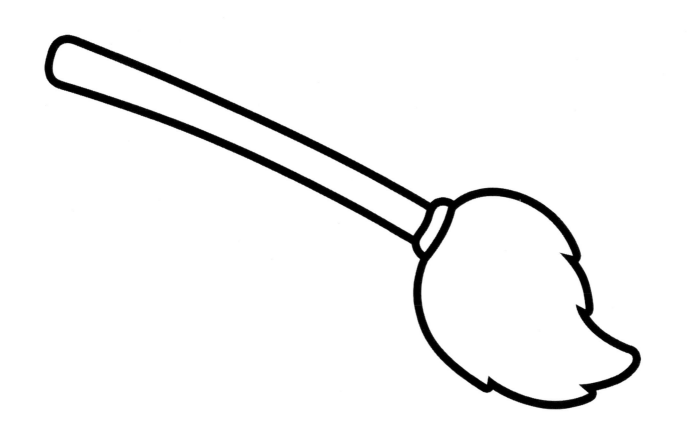

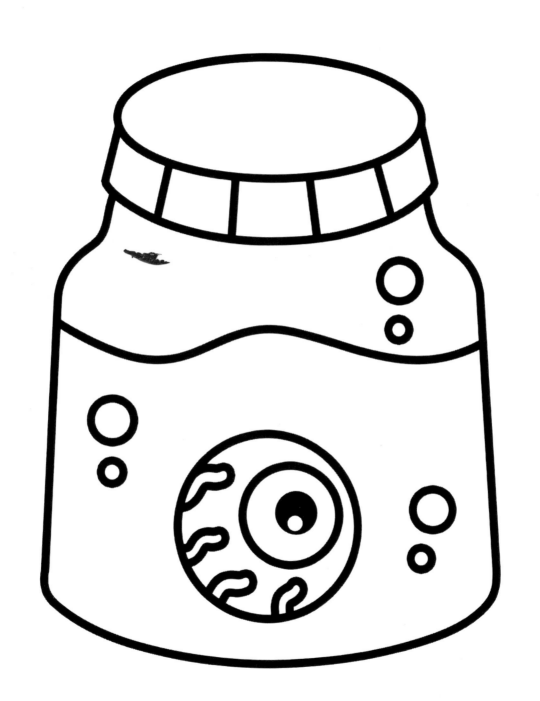

Made in United States
North Haven, CT
28 October 2024

59507324R00057